In her gracious and captiv[...] [...]
our most fragile and vulnerable places to [...]
great love towards us. Through four seemingly obscure, unnamed women of the Bible and their inspiring testimonies of faith, Michelle compels us to draw closer, dig deeper, and grow stronger so that we can live our own testimonies of faith wherever God has called us. You will be blessed!

- Lisa Murray, Licensed Marriage and Family Therapist, author of *Peace For A Lifetime*

Women need women for encouragement and example. If we're honest, many of us feel unnoticed and unappreciated in a world clamoring to be noticed. We find ourselves feeling as if we are making no significant contribution to the world. We feel unnamed. There is no better place to find real women living real lives than in God's Word, and how encouraging it is to find *unnamed* women of the Bible offering us modern women the examples we need today. Michelle does a beautiful work of extracting and sharing these stories, along with her own, and bringing each one to life as the women they were: women used by God for His glory who, without ever being named, impact future generations. This study is relevant for every woman in every demographic and age group, particularly those who struggle with identity. Michelle gives us an opportunity to dive into the lives and lessons of women who have walked before us, unnamed and yet very used by God.

- Lori Macmath, owner of *Internet Café Devotions*

From the foreword of this book, I was drawn in to complexities of "unnamed women" of the Bible that I had never thought of before. Michelle has a way of making me feel that my own life was significant and important to God the Father through her explanation of seemingly insignificant characters we sometimes gloss over. She also weaves in her own relatable testimonies with total humility, which made me trust her wisdom even more. I highly recommend this devotional.

- Suzanne Bowen, founder of Suzanne Bowen Fitness

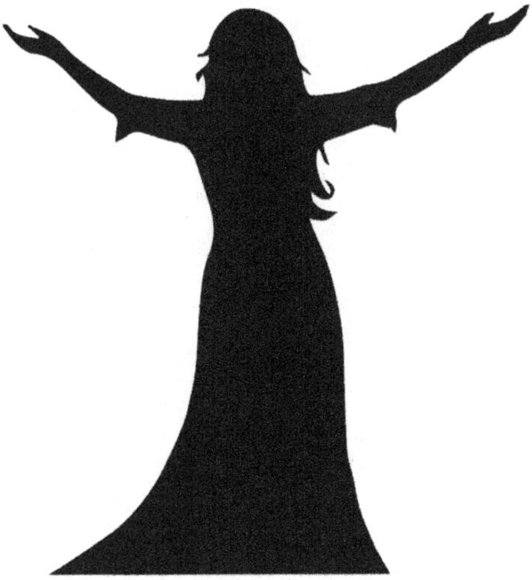

Unnamed Women of the Bible

Lessons of Value, Belonging, and Worth

Michelle Discavage

UNNAMED WOMEN OF THE BIBLE
Copyright © 2016 Michelle Discavage. All rights reserved.

ISBN 978-1522790280
Subject headings: WOMEN/BIBLE STUDY/SPIRITUAL LIFE

Unless otherwise noted, Scripture quotations are taken from THE HOLY BIBLE, NEW INTERNATIONAL VERSION®, NIV®, copyright © 1973, 1978, 1984, 2011 by Biblica, Inc.® Used by permission. All rights reserved worldwide.

Scripture quotations marked NASB are taken from the New American Standard Bible®, copyright © 1960, 1962, 1963, 1968, 1971, 1972, 1973, 1975, 1977, 1995 by the Lockman Foundation. Used by permission.

Scripture quotations marked NLT are taken from the Holy Bible, New Living Translation, copyright © 1996, 2004, 2007 by Tyndale House Foundation. Used by permission of Tyndale House Publishers, Inc., Carol Stream, Illinois 60188. All rights reserved.

Printed in the United States of America

For my daughter, Zoe. May you always be assured of God's love for you and of your place in His kingdom. Thank you for teaching me how valuable we truly are and for inspiring me every single day.

Table of Contents

Introduction   1

Week 1: The Woman with the Issue of Bleeding   4

  Day 1: The I Am Says I Am   8

  Day 2: God Sees You   13

  Day 3: God Hears You   16

  Day 4: God Will Restore You   20

  Day 5: The Beauty of Humility   25

Week 2: The Shunammite Woman   29

  Day 1: A Servant's Heart   33

  Day 2: Contentment   36

  Day 3: Grieve but Believe   41

  Day 4: Remember What He Has Done   47

  Day 5: Share Your Story   52

Week 3: The Wise Woman of Abel	55
Day 1: What's in Your Heart?	58
Day 2: Words Matter	63
Day 3: Know Your Motivation	67
Day 4: Gifts Are to Be Used	72
Day 5: Be at Peace	77
Week 4: The Widow and the Jars of Oil	83
Day 1: Bring the Jars	87
Day 2: The Obedience Blessing	93
Day 3: Ask for Help	97
Day 4: He Will Equip You	101
Day 5: Community Wins	104
A Final Word	108
Discussion Guide	109
Acknowledgements	113
Notes	116

INTRODUCTION

In 2013 I attended a Bible study entitled, "Road Signs: Stories of Relentless Trust and Extravagant Love," written and taught by Paige Allen. This eight-week study was extraordinary and launched me into writing this book. At the close of "Road Signs," Paige asked a few women in attendance to speak on lesser-known women of the Bible. As one of those selected, I was excited to dive in and discover which woman I would speak on.

I was drawn to the woman and the jars of oil (2 Kings 4:1-7). After sharing what I had learned from studying this woman, I wondered what lessons could be discovered from the stories of other unnamed women in the Bible. I began to research and published many of my findings on my website www.SparkedLiving.net. For months I toyed with the idea of turning these posts into a Bible study. Yet it was not until my husband mentioned it as well that I began to take action.

This four-week study is one I have prayed about and pondered for well over a year. I realize now that God began writing this book each time I sat down to write a blog post. There have been moments I have questioned my ability to accomplish this. I have had a multitude of doubts and fears. But God used these women whose names I do not know to encourage me to press on.

Above all I hope this study speaks to women of their value and worth as God's daughters. I believe women are struggling with identity and with finding their confidence in Christ. My prayer is for each woman who reads this to be drawn into the fullness of God's love. Be assured He knows your name, He knows everything about you, and He loves you deeply. You are accepted and deeply cherished.

Week 1

THE WOMAN WITH THE ISSUE OF BLEEDING

And He said to her, "Daughter, your faith has made you well; go in peace." — Luke 8:48

Three surgeries in three years, a case of mono, and the discovery of extreme food sensitivities left me depleted. And my weight. Up and down like a never-ending yo-yo. I became exhausted and frustrated. Every day felt like I faced the same battle. I switched doctors, tried alternative methods, and looked beyond traditional medicine in hopes of healing my damaged body. I watched as others seemed to live full exciting lives while I struggled to merely get out of bed and shower each day.

Luke 8 tells a well-known story about a woman with an issue of blood. For twelve years she suffered but with just one touch of Jesus' robe, she is healed. Instantly, over a decade of suffering comes to an end. Beautiful, isn't it?

This woman who is not even given a name is alone. At this time and in this culture, women were not highly valued. They had few rights and were subject to the choices of the men around them. As a woman who was unmarried, this woman would not have had a strong place in society.

Not only is she a woman all alone, but she is also a woman who has an issue of blood. Most likely she suffered menstrual bleeding. (Just try to wrap your brain around a twelve-year menstrual cycle!) According to Jewish law, she would be deemed unclean. For twelve years, anything and anyone whom she touched would also be unclean. She was by all accounts an outcast in society. She would have ranked somewhere among the lepers. Due to the strict laws regarding blood, after her bleeding ceased, she would have to offer a sacrifice of two pigeons and two turtles and then take part in a ritual-cleansing bath known as a *mikveh*. In addition, an unclean woman could not be married. She would be cast aside, left alone. There would be no one to speak for her, to care for her, to protect her, or provide for her.

However, she knows if she can just get close to Jesus she will be healed. Surely, even on the outskirts of society, she has heard the stories of Jesus. While I am not certain how, this woman has extraordinary faith that Jesus is able to heal her. She is aware that she will have to fight the crowds in spite of how she may feel or any weakness she may be experiencing. Despite being cast aside as unclean, she must push through in order to receive healing.

Alone for twelve years, she gets through the crowd, touches the fringe of His cloak, and is instantly healed. She does not approach Him face to face. She simply tries to go unnoticed, as she usually does in her daily life, to get to Jesus. She is certain that He can heal her but does not expect Him to speak to her. It is not easy. The crowds follow Jesus closely, and no one will be there to clear a path for her.

Jesus stops immediately, asking who touched Him. Frustrated, Peter says it could have been anyone. Jesus replies that someone did touch Him because the "power had gone out" of Him. The woman, unnoticed and cast aside for twelve years, cannot avoid this confrontation. Trembling, falling before Him, she admits it was her. With a shaking voice, she explains why she touched Him and how she was instantly healed. The crowd that would have declared her unfit in any other setting now witnessed how Jesus healed her with only one touch.

This woman, who has had no place to belong, who is not even given a name, hears Jesus call her "Daughter." He gives her an identity and the position of daughter. He is letting her know He

Week 1: The Woman with the Issue of Bleeding

will fight for her. For twelve years she has been left to care for herself but now Jesus steps in, "*your faith has made you well; go in peace.*" In one statement, He accepts her, encourages her, and esteems her. The unclean is made clean. The one who would not be accepted in society is now a part of Jesus' family. She has a place to belong, Someone who will stand beside her.

My own struggles with achieving optimal health continue. I do not have all the answers, but I am confident in the One who does. It was only when I began praying, when I asked for wisdom and direction concerning doctors to visit, that I started to feel a bit more normal. I am now surrounded by a supportive team, one that prays for wisdom and discernment in finding the path to my healing.

At the core of every woman, I believe there is a need for someone to fight for us. Why else would we be drawn to fairy tales? We each desire a knight in shining armor to come slay the dragons threatening to destroy us. Women want to feel connected, a part of something outside of ourselves. We have a need to be adored and loved, cherished without conditions. We desire someone to draw us out of the crowd, someone to ensure we are safe.

I want to encourage you today, those of you who feel there is no champion standing in your corner. There is a Champion, the greatest there will ever be, interceding on your behalf. He spreads His arms wide, beckoning you to come. You may have to push through the crowd; you may have to struggle and fight your way to Him. I cannot say the road will be easy, but as you simply sit in His presence you will hear him say, "*Daughter, you are mine. I have loved you with an everlasting love. I will fight for you. You belong here."*

DAY 1: THE I AM SAYS I AM

Read Luke 8:48. By what name does Jesus call the woman?

How might this one statement have altered her life after having been a social outcast for twelve years?

    In this passage, the Greek word *thygatér* is a term of endearment toward a younger woman, by extension meaning "daughter." When Jesus calls this woman daughter, He shows He cares for her.

    Knowing what God says of us is vital to living the life that He desires for us. Society told this woman she was unclean, unwanted, an outcast. With one word, Jesus overrides every negative name she has been given by renaming her *Daughter*.

What names has the world given to you? What effect do these terms have on you?

"You are fat. You will never have a boyfriend." I was told those things in college. In high school a volleyball coach belittled me in a gym full of people, letting me know I would certainly never be good enough to play for her. In middle school a relative, who was blessed with a tall lean figure, exclaimed how large my thighs were. Around the same time, a gymnastics coach shouted my failures for all to hear as I stood on a balance beam fighting tears.

Words hurt. That is what I learned. I cannot fully recall when I began learning this lesson, but it was one I learned all too well. Words can make a person feel small and uncared for and worthless.

I believed the words being spoken to me and those that had been spoken to me in the past. I saw myself as unlovable, unattractive, and unworthy.

With the help of a life coach I began to overcome the lies that I had heard. Like the woman with the issue of blood, I felt like an outcast. I felt unwanted and unwelcomed. But God beautifully and wonderfully began to rewrite the story, and I began to listen.

One of the powerful tools I was given to overcome the words that hurt me was to write the truth to defeat each lie that entered my mind. This powerful exercise will begin unleashing truth in your life. Take your time; do not rush through this. We are going to break free today.

Write the lies you have believed about yourself. Then, replace each lie with the truth of God's Word. Pray for God to show you the truth as you pore over Scripture or use lyrics from a worship song. As the Bible says, the Truth will set you free.

The World Says:	God Says:

Use this exercise as often as you need and keep your list close by. The more we fill our minds with truth, the less room we will have for the lies attempting to destroy us.

What else does God say about us? Let's continue looking at the names God has given us:

John 1:12

Ephesians 1:5

Romans 15:7

Romans 6:6

Genesis 1:27 says we have been created in what?

1 Peter 2:9

Psalm 17:8

In Isaiah 62:4 the term *Hephzibah* is used, which means, "my delight is in her." **Friend, God's delight is in each of us.** He has called us Daughter and prepared a place for us. We are welcome. We are treasured and deeply loved.

Our loving Savior is fully aware of us, of our need for Him. As He did with the woman with the issue of bleeding, as we reach out to Him for His healing touch, He is turning to face us, reaching out, and telling us we belong.

The I AM has declared I am His daughter, as are you. Write out a prayer of thanksgiving asking Him to help you overcome any lies that may be hindering you.

DAY 2: GOD SEES YOU

I was running late and I had no one to blame but myself. The meeting would already be starting when I arrived. I snuck in the back door, hoping to go unnoticed. My plan worked, at least until I tripped and sent my bag flying through the air. My intention was to sneak in quietly but instead those around me were asking if I was okay. So much for my career as a stealthy ninja. Rather than a silent entry I made a loud, "Here I am!" entrance.

Read Luke 8:44. From which direction did the woman approach Jesus?

Hoping to go unnoticed, the woman with the issue of blood approaches from behind Jesus. Yet Jesus turns, asking who touched Him.

Have you ever felt unnoticed? Have you ever hoped to be unnoticed? Describe what this was, or is, like for you.

If you are a parent you have most likely heard the words, "watch me." Whether she is dancing, making a face, or climbing on playground equipment, my own daughter often asks me to watch her. If I divert my eyes even slightly, she will walk over, look me in the eyes and state, "Mom, watch me until I tell you to stop." She wants to be noticed, especially by her father and me. I have realized that I am much the same. Yes, I want to be noticed by others, but more importantly I want to know God notices me.

Describe a time you felt noticed by God. How did this change your perception of Him?

Read the following passages and write down what each passage says God does.

Zephaniah 3:17

Zephaniah 3:15

Isaiah 62:5

In Isaiah 62:5, the Hebrew word for "rejoice" means joy, delight, or celebration. The Creator throws a holy party for us, my friend! In a time when we often feel alone and unnoticed, even when we try to hide, God rejoices over and celebrates us. He calls us by name and celebrates.

I believe He wants us to know how deep His joy for us is. He notices us when we feel unlovable, unworthy, un-everything and delights in us. Does that not make your spirit soar? I cannot help but smile knowing God sees me.

What does it mean to you to know that God sees or notices you?

Write out your own prayer, thanking God for calling you by name, for rejoicing over you with singing, and for noticing you. Take a moment and allow Him to wash over you and rest in His presence, in the arms of our Father.

Week 1: The Woman with the Issue of Bleeding

DAY 3: GOD HEARS YOU

With her hands clasped around my face, my daughter looked directly at me, "Mom, I need you to listen to me! Please focus." When I explained I had been listening, she simply responded, "But your eyes are not on me. I want your full attention." While a bit bossy at a young age, she was right. I was hearing every word she said but I was not giving her my full attention.

Read Luke 8:47-48.

Jesus responds to the woman after she states why she touched Him and has declared her healing.

Have you ever felt ignored by others? By God? Explain as much as you are comfortable with.

The woman in Luke 8, whom Christ called Daughter, was more than likely accustomed to not being heard because she lived in isolation. Due to her condition, she would have been excluded from society. Like being unnoticed, feeling ignored is equally painful.

As imperfect humans, we are not always good listeners. We do not always take the time to listen or truly hear what others are saying. With our frequently hectic lifestyles, we are not often prone to slowing down our pace to take part in conversations. However, God is always willing to hear from His children. Scripture tells us how He loves to hear from us.

Read the following verses, writing down key phrases that show God hears us.

Psalm 3:4

Psalm 18:6

Psalm 34:15

Psalm 55:16-17

Romans 10:13

Week 1: The Woman with the Issue of Bleeding 17

1 John 5:14-15

After reading these verses, how does your belief that God hears us change?

A friend from college and I can sit and talk well into the evening hours. Much like we did twenty years ago, we lose track of time and become so wrapped up in our conversation that we have to force ourselves to stop. We enjoy our time together and our conversations because we allow each other the space to speak. We do not interrupt. We ask a few poignant questions. We feel heard by one another. I imagine you have a friend like that as well.

Tell about a time you felt heard. What was it like to know the other person was truly interested in what you were saying?

On a scale of 1-10, how would you rate your listening skills? Are you able to listen without formulating a response, or without impatiently waiting your turn to interject?

Knowing our words are not falling on deaf ears is freeing and reassuring. We feel cared for when another person will cease all distractions and focus on us. This simple act causes us to feel special.

Unlike you and me, God consistently listens. He does not get distracted. He focuses His attention on us and hears every word we utter. He hears the cries of our heart. Yes, sister, I know prayers can sometimes feel as if they are bouncing off the ceiling or not being heard. But rest assured, in complete faith, He does hear.

Whatever is on your heart, your mind, talk to God about it. Spend some time praying and speak whatever comes to you to say. Our prayers do not need to be eloquent: they need only be spoken.

DAY 4: GOD WILL RESTORE YOU

Is there an area of your life in which you feel broken? Stuck? Have lost hope?

I have been there. For years, I never felt I was enough. I did not measure up. It seemed that more often than not I fell short. I fell short of my goals, of expectations, of what others wanted from me. Did I truly lack so much?

It was painful and lonely. I knew there was more to the story, to my story. I knew what God had poured into me through the mentors He placed in my life. Was it all to be forgotten? Maybe I was fooling myself. Maybe I was passed over because I was not the leader I believed myself to be.

Three surgeries in three years along with various illnesses had left me depleted. Physically I was exhausted. Mentally and emotionally I faked sanity and confidence. Spiritually I was begging God to open a door, any door, for me to move forward. The stagnant life was not for me, yet there I remained.

When I felt I might crumble, an unexpected hand reached out. One phone call held the answer God had been preparing for me. I was presented with an opportunity to use the gifts and strengths God instilled in me.

A surprising voice spoke life into the darkened places. Hope was revived in what God said through this person. For the task ahead, I was enough. I was the one who was needed. One phone call restored every broken place overwhelming me.

In her healing, the woman in Luke 8 is restored to society. She is no longer unclean. Yes, she will remember those twelve years. However, she will no longer be the woman *with* an issue of bleeding. Instead she will be the woman who *had* an issue of bleeding. She will be *Daughter*.

Are you praying a prayer of healing? If so, write out as much of your prayer as you are comfortable with.

Throughout the Bible, we see God healing. In fact, the story of the woman with the issue of blood is tucked inside another story of physical restoration.

Read Luke 8:40-42 and Luke 8:49-56. Who approaches Jesus? Why? What happens?

Week 1: The Woman with the Issue of Bleeding

Isn't it lovely? In the midst of going to heal Jairus' daughter, to restore this young girl to life, Jesus stops and heals the woman He calls daughter.

Have you experienced God's healing? Share your story.

Let's explore other stories of God's restoration. Read the following verses and write any notes on the passages that stand out to you.

Deuteronomy 30:1-4

Joel 2:25-26

Jeremiah 30:17

2 Corinthians 5:17

Psalm 51:1-2, 6-12

Restoration is the heart of God. Since sin entered the Garden of Eden, God has been restoring His creation to Himself. His promises are always kept.

Luke 18:38 tells us a blind man called out as Jesus was approaching Jericho, "*Jesus, Son of David, have mercy on me!*" The man is told to be quiet by those leading the way. Something must have been stirring within this blind beggar because he called out again, "*Son of David, have mercy on me!*"

Father, help us to have the same relentless pursuit of you. Others would have us stop. The story continues. Jesus stopped the procession and had the unseeing man brought to Him. Jesus asked one question, "*What do you want me to do for you?*" The blind man had but one request, "*Lord, I want to regain my sight!*" (Luke 18:41)

How often have you been stopped by the crowd? How often have you not drawn near to Him because there were too many distractions?

"*Receive your sight, your faith has made you well,*" Jesus responded. Instantly, the man was no longer blind. With his sight restored he began following Jesus and worshiping God.

Week 1: The Woman with the Issue of Bleeding

Do you ever have trouble seeing God at work in your life?

I cannot promise complete healing. Do I believe God is able to? Yes. Will He? I do not know. I do know, beyond a shadow of a doubt, there will come a day we will be fully restored. We will worship at the throne of Christ without hindrance. There will be no more disease, no more failings, no more tears. There will only be a body of believers restored to their Creator.

Join me in praying:

Father, You are good and worthy of all praise. Open our eyes to see You more. Give us eyes to see the work You have done and are doing in our lives. Help us to see You in the everyday and stir our hearts to rejoice in You. We believe You are able to restore us, to heal us, and ask You to do so. May we follow after You in relentless pursuit. Amen.

DAY 5: THE BEAUTY OF HUMILITY

"It's humbling," she said, "I am in a room with this powerful substance, just me and this machine, and Jesus. No one else can be in there because the radiation used to help me can be harmful. Interesting, isn't it? I feel so small during my treatments. I see my own lack very clearly. I can do nothing but lie there, and pray, and worship. So many times I longed for a quiet place to talk to Him, free of interruptions. I have it now, I suppose. I am humbled each time because God always meets me there. I can feel His presence. I have never felt so small, yet so safe. This cancer may end up killing me but I would not trade it."

My dear friend met her Savior face to face less than a year after our conversation. She taught me so much about humility during our time together.

In day two of this week's study, we discussed how the woman in Luke 8 approached Jesus from behind. She does not face Him until He turns to her. This woman knows merely touching His robe will heal her.

Read Luke 8:47.

What does the woman do when she realizes she won't go unnoticed?

Not only do I see a woman desperate to be healed, but I also see a woman who possesses great humility.

In your own words, define humility.

In Hebrew, humility is an extension of acting in a cautious manner, of stooping down (see Proverbs 15:33). In Greek, humility includes modesty, gentleness, and meekness (see Colossians 3:12 and 1 Peter 5:5).

Another definition of humility is *an attitude of mind that realizes one is without reason for distinction in God's sight.*

Read Proverbs 11:2. According to this passage, what is with the humble?

Read Micah 6:8. What does the Lord require? Why?

Read James 1:19-21. At the end of the passage, what are we to accept? How?

There have been too many times I have tried to forge ahead on my own. With pride leading the way, I was certain I would obtain success on my own. Even when circumstances overwhelmed me, when I felt everything was crumbling around me, I would hold fast to the notion I did not need help from anyone. How wrong I was. Pride makes a poor travel companion and often complicates the journey or derails it altogether. If I have learned anything, it is how desperately I need to reach out for help.

We need the Lord. We cannot, contrary to public opinion, live completely independent lives. It is for us, for our souls, we are called to humility. When we understand what God has done on our behalf, we see our great need for Him. We will come to see we have nothing to boast of outside of Him. Our very best cannot measure up to Him. It is because of Him we are able.

Is pride interfering with your ability to approach Christ? Others? Pray for God to show you areas in need of being cleared of pride. Ask His forgiveness. Ask Him to show you how to walk humbly before Him and with Him.

Week 2

The Shunammite Woman

One day Elisha went to Shunem. And a well-to-do woman was there, who urged him to stay for a meal. So whenever he came by, he stopped there to eat. She said to her husband, "I know that this man who often comes our way is a holy man of God. Let's make a small room on the roof and put in it a bed and a table, a chair and a lamp for him. Then he can stay there whenever he comes to us." — 2 Kings 4:8-10

After several failed rounds of fertility treatments, my friend, Amanda, and her husband chose to move forward with adoption. Two children were welcomed into their home as she was told the possibility of conceiving on her own was extremely low. Years later, her son prayed before their Christmas dinner, asking for a sibling. My friend gently explained his request was not possible, though the idea was wonderful. Three months later, a positive pregnancy test proved everyone wrong. Their daughter was born via C-section a month earlier than expected and spent almost a month in the hospital's NICU before going home. What doctors claimed was impossible, God made possible.

2 Kings 4 tells of a Shunammite woman and her husband who provide a room for Elisha, the prophet, to stay in each time he travels through their city. Upon one particular visit, Elisha considers what can be done for this woman who has shown him kindness.

She is old, and without a son. Elisha calls her and prophesies, "*In one year, a son will be born to you.*" She is a woman who has not complained, saying she has a home among her own people when asked what can be done for her.

How her heart must have skipped when she heard him speak of a son to be born to her.

"*Do not mislead me, my heart could not take it.*"

Just as Elisha said, a son is born the following year. The child grows and joins his father in the field with the reapers until one day pain takes hold of him. "*My head, Father, my head.*"

As she holds the son who had been promised her in her lap, he dies. The heart that skipped at the news of having the child for whom she always longed, now skips with grief. Laying her son on the bed made for Elisha, this grieving mother saddles a donkey and heads to the prophet. In spite of the pain gripping her she says, "*Everything is all right.*"

Then she falls at Elisha's feet, "*Did I not say to not raise my hopes?*" Losing a son she once held in her arms is more painful than never holding a son at all.

She leads Elisha to the place where the boy lies. While she waits outside the room, he closes the door and prays to the Lord. Covering the boy with himself, Elisha breathes life into the son so deeply loved. Sneezing seven times, the boy returns to life. His mother enters, bowing again at Elisha's feet. She turns to walk away with the son who was promised to her. Elisha then warns her of a coming famine.

Heeding Elisha's warning of the coming famine, the woman and her family sojourn. They return seven years later to find their land is claimed by others. She shares with the king what Elisha did for her, "*I was barren, and as Elisha promised, I bore a son. My son fell ill and died. Elisha restored him to life.*" Hearing her account, the king restores her land.

In the midst of emotional upheaval, this woman, whose name we do not know, remains obedient.

Using the resources given to her, she allows a wandering prophet a place to lay his head. When he speaks of life or famine, she listens; she does as she is asked. And yet, she teaches us that **obedience does not mean the road will be easy.** While her story ends in blessing and an incredible testimony, I do not imagine that in the middle, as her son lay lifeless in her arms, she felt like rejoicing.

Instead, she runs to the one who can help.

What do you do? What do we do when a promise we have been told seems to be ripped out of our grasp? Do we turn and run to the One who spoke the promise? Or do we scream that life is unjust, and surely it was never meant to be anyway? Do we ask for help? Do we humble ourselves to the point of kneeling down to the One who created us? Or do we complain to any ears that will listen?

An unnamed woman, known only by the place she is from, instructs us. When you see a need that you are able to meet, do so. Rejoice in the promises given to you. Run to the One who spoke the promises, even when they seem to be falling away. Walk in obedience, even if you must leave your place of comfort. Share your story with others.

When those promises are given, the ones that seem too big to believe, hold on. God is writing an incredible story for you.

DAY 1: A SERVANT'S HEART

Read 2 Kings 4:9-10.

I become busy, as I am sure you do too. When busyness has overtaken me, I do not notice the needs of others. With errands to run, mouths to feed, a to-do list to accomplish, I easily miss when someone else is in need. But the Shunammite woman? She notices the prophet and addresses a need he has.

Describe a time you filled a need for someone else, not because they asked, but because you saw what was needed.

What motivated you to fill this need?

Why is serving others important (apart from the fact that God says to do so)?

Week 2: The Shunammite Woman

Read Romans 12:9-13.

Serving others is the best expression of love. As we serve one another, we are glorifying Christ.

Read Matthew 20:25-28. According to verse 26, the great among you shall be what?

Greatness is not ruling over others, but serving them. Like Christ, we are to serve. We become more like Him through our service. Can we ever serve the way Christ did? No. In the ultimate act of service, He offered Himself as a sacrifice for our sins.

Because of Christ's love for us, and His work in us, His love will flow out of us as we serve one another.

In what ways is God calling you to serve?

Pray to be sensitive to where God wants you to serve. Ask Him to reveal this to you. In the space provided, write your prayer, and what you believe God is guiding you to do.

DAY 2: CONTENTMENT

Read 2 Kings 4:11-13.

How does the woman respond when asked what can be done for her?

Describe her attitude.

As I read through these passages, the Shunammite woman seems to be content. Elisha, the man of God this woman has cared for, asks what can be done for her. She makes no request.

How many times have we been asked what can be done for us? It is not difficult for me to think of a long list of ways to return a favor, whether I voice them or not. The problem is that we, as women, can be quiet about our own needs. Regardless of the circumstances, or the depth of our need, we often do not speak up.

While our hearts are pounding and our soul's desire longs to be shouted out, we remain quiet.

Maybe you have a hard time speaking up when you have a need.

Do you tend to be quick to list what can be done for you, or do you have a hard time admitting your needs? Why do you think you do this?

Read 2 Kings 4:14.

What is missing in this woman's life?

Being childless meant the family's name would end and their land and possessions would pass on to others. It was a bitter disappointment to be without children. Yet, this woman does not complain and makes no request. Whether she found the idea of having children to be impossible I cannot say. I am struck by her contentment.

Week 2: The Shunammite Woman

There is quite a bit of talk about contentment and how to live a content life. This seems to be elusive for many, but should it be? In all honesty, I do not think so. We live in a society that glorifies busyness. As long as we can answer, "I am just so busy" when asked how we are, we are satisfied. Sister, we are missing true contentment.

G.K. Chesterton said, "True contentment is a real, even an active, virtue—not only affirmative but creative. It is the power of getting out of any situation all there is in it." [1]

Perspective matters and contentment is directly related to our perspective. I have noticed in my life how true this is. During setbacks with my health, I became unsettled and antsy as I focused on how far off my goals seemed. The further away I was from meeting them, the more discontent I became. As I focused more on who God is rather than my own abilities, my feelings of discontentment subsided. God never changes. He keeps every promise. I can be content in who He is.

Read Philippians 4:10-13. In your own words, what does Paul say is the secret to being content?

Paul knows Christ is the way to contentment. Through imprisonments and beatings, as well as in times of plenty, Paul has learned his contentment comes from Christ. It is through Christ that Paul is able to endure all he has experienced in his life.

Read 2 Corinthians 4:13-18. What are we to fix our eyes on and why?

We are finite beings in the hands of an infinite God. He has prepared a place for us in eternity. This life will pass away. Yes, there are days that will threaten to destroy us. There will be circumstances in our lives causing our hearts to break and our faith to waver. For the believer, however, there is also hope. There is a hope-filled perspective we can adopt to endure all situations. We can find contentment when we walk alongside our Heavenly Father.

What are ways you spend time with God in order to deepen your relationship with Him?

If you are currently in a situation causing you discontentment, take a moment to pray. Write down your prayer, if you would like. Share with our loving Father your desire to find contentment in the midst of your circumstances and ask for guidance in how to do so. Trust Him: He is faithful.

DAY 3: GRIEVE BUT BELIEVE

One Wednesday in January 2015, my husband and I walked out of the children's emergency room with our daughter. A febrile seizure during her lunch period resulted in an ambulance ride to the hospital and a multitude of tests. Receiving the call that my child had suffered a seizure and was being taken to the ER was horrifying. Somewhere in my mind, I knew she would be okay, but this was my baby, my one and only child. As her mother, I wanted nothing more than to hold my sweet girl in my arms, to stroke her hair and whisper how much I love her.

Five hours after being admitted, we were sent home. We were hungry, tired, and incredibly thankful. As we crossed the parking lot, her hand in mine, I was reminded of a Wednesday eleven years prior.

My sister and her husband left Houston Children's Hospital after having to release their son to eternity. His one year of life involved multiple heart surgeries. On this day, however, their hearts broke in ways they never had known before. I watched my family walk through the most devastating moment we had ever known.

Read 2 Kings 4:18-21.

Week 2: The Shunammite Woman

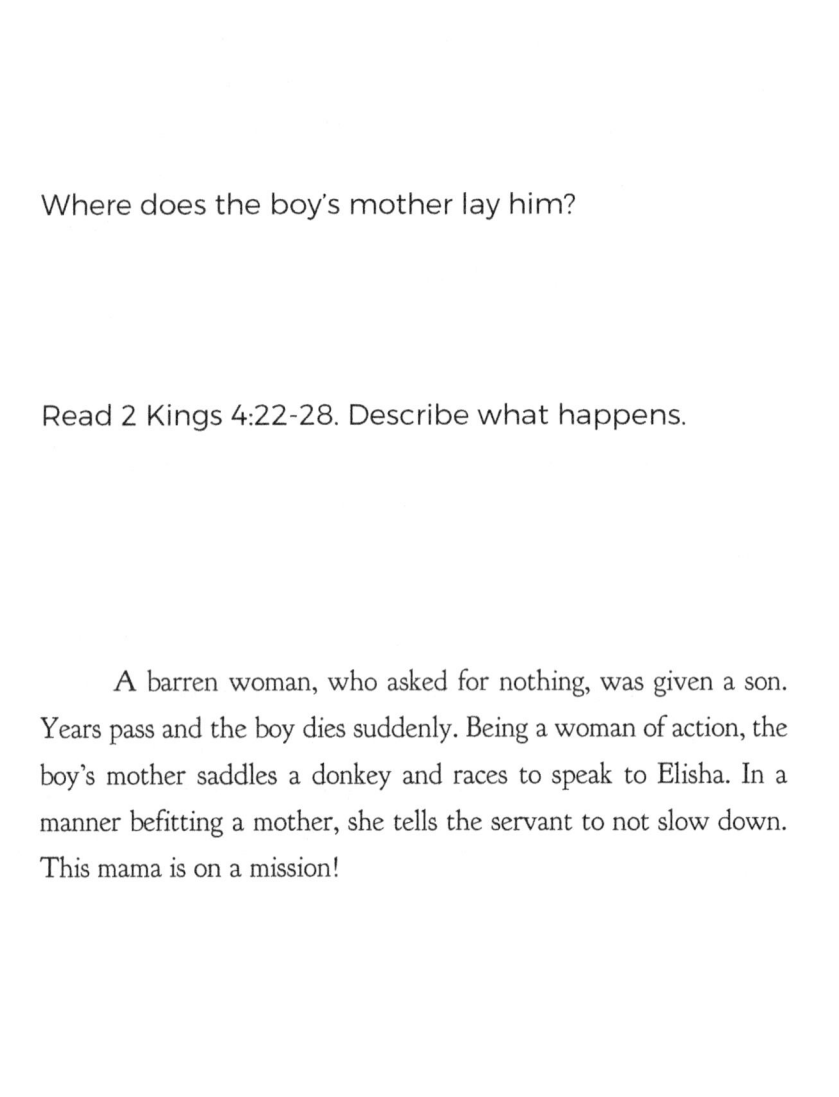

What happens in these passages?

Where does the boy's mother lay him?

Read 2 Kings 4:22-28. Describe what happens.

    A barren woman, who asked for nothing, was given a son. Years pass and the boy dies suddenly. Being a woman of action, the boy's mother saddles a donkey and races to speak to Elisha. In a manner befitting a mother, she tells the servant to not slow down. This mama is on a mission!

Have you experienced a time where you charged full steam ahead, completely focused on where you needed to go? Explain below.

How were you feeling at this time? Was your heart rate elevated? Were you out of breath? Describe your physiological reactions.

In her haste to speak to Elisha, did you catch her response? Look at 2 Kings 4:26. When asked if everything is all right, she says it is. What? Her son has died and she's charging to Mt. Carmel, yet she says, "*Everything is all right.*" When she approaches Elisha, she falls at his feet.

This brokenhearted mama shows what it means to grieve but believe. I can almost hear her yelling the words in verse 28. "*Did I ask you for a son, my lord? Didn't I tell you, 'Don't raise my hopes'?*"

Elisha promised her a son, and yet in the midst of her grief, she refuses to leave Elisha.

Are you praying for a miracle? Have you started to let go of the promise God has given you or are you still holding on?

Read 2 Kings 4:32-37.

God partners with Elisha to bring the boy back to life. The same one who promised the child now restores the child to life. Again, the child's mother bows at Elisha's feet: this time, in humble praise.

As we all know grief never ends. There is no twelve-step process for grief recovery. There are many days I wonder how my sister and her husband have made it through each day. Their exact journey is their story to tell, but hope is at the center of their heartache. My sister shared a quote by Rob Bell that sums up how to grieve while believing well, "Ultimately our gift to the world around us is hope. Not blind hope that pretends everything is fine… but the kind of hope that comes from staring suffering right in the eyes and refusing to believe that this is all there is. It is what we all need - hope that comes not from going around suffering but from going through it." [2]

Read 1 Thessalonians 4:13-14. What promise provides hope?

Read Psalm 130:5. According to this psalm, where should our hope be placed?

Read Ephesians 1:17-21. How do these verses encourage you?

Not every situation turns out the way we would like. As much as I would love to offer you the perfect prayer to ensure loved ones are healed, horrible situations are avoided, and that all will be well this side of Heaven, I cannot. I can encourage you to continue to press into Christ. In Him, through Him, and because of Him we can have hope in spite of the most heartbreaking circumstances.

I know some of you are in the midst of a situation threatening to unravel every fiber of your being. While I cannot ease your burden or suffering, I know the One who can. I encourage you to pour out your heart to Him. Cry, scream, be angry, be confused, be hurt. It is okay, sister, God can take all those emotions. He can bear every burden you carry. He can hear your angry cries and love you still. Rest in Him. Grieve but believe. Pray with me, would you?

Father, you are good. You created the heavens and all that is in them. You created humanity in Your own image and You know us fully. You know our hurts, our struggles, and the situations causing our faith to waver. Comfort those who mourn. Reveal beauty for ashes and speak Your love over those who feel You are far away. Thank You for the peace that surpasses understanding, for unending love, and hope that does not disappoint. Amen.

DAY 4: REMEMBER WHAT HE HAS DONE

In 2010, I joined a group from our former Nashville church to study the Bible in Israel. To be there, to study, to see places spoken of in the Bible was mind-blowing. We walked in the wilderness; we climbed Masada; we journeyed to Bethlehem; we were taught in a vineyard; we sat on the Temple steps overlooking Jerusalem. It was a trip I had only dreamed of but there I was in Jericho, Jerusalem, and the Valley of Elah. I waded into the Dead Sea and the Mediterranean. I sailed on the Sea of Galilee, and prayed at the Wailing Wall.

In times of stress or confusion, I often find myself mentally returning to Israel. The sounds, the sights, the people, the lessons. Instantly, I remember what God did in a span of two weeks. I remember how He made the trip possible. I remember how He met me there.

Read 2 Kings 8:1-8.

What did Elisha instruct the Shunammite woman's family to do? Why?

A seven-year famine is coming, and Elisha warns the Shunammite woman and her family to leave. Notice her response. Nowhere do I read she called her closest friends to pray. She does not spread the word to her neighbors and ask their opinion. She and her family go. They head toward Philistine country and remain there for the duration of the famine.

Has there been a time you felt called to do something involving a big change? How did you respond? Were you quick to act or did you hesitate?

The Shunammite woman encourages me because she is quick to act. Me? I want to try to see the whole picture before embarking on a new adventure. I make lists. I weigh pros and cons. My mind hosts a great debate on the matter. Rather than dive right in to where faith calls me, I am prone to wade safely on shore.

Remember, this woman who had been barren gave birth to a son. Her son later died but Elisha restored the boy to life. The Shunammite woman knew she could trust Elisha's word. He had

48 *Unnamed Women of the Bible*

already fulfilled the promises he had spoken to her. Her experience gave her the ability to trust Elisha's word.

Record a time God came through for you. Use the space below to recall a good work God did on your behalf, one you or others thought impossible.

Is our faith so weak or are we so forgetful? I began keeping a prayer journal a few years ago in order to help me remember what God has done. My blog also serves as a reminder. I often become so caught up in current circumstances I tend to forget all God has already done in my life. In my forgetfulness, my fears and doubts increase.

Read the following:

Joshua 24:16-18

Psalm 105:5

Galatians 1:6-7

The disciples forgot. As Jesus is being crucified, most of the disciples have scattered. The men who walked alongside Jesus, saw with their own eyes the miracles Jesus performed, the ones who shared in the Last Supper, ran. They forgot. In the moment, their minds did not recall all Jesus did or all He promised. Their fears and doubts welled up and off they went.

We will forget too. We will be prone to freak-outs because we are not quick to remind ourselves what God has already done. Our temporal minds have trouble grasping an eternal God. But, sister, God does not forget.

Why is remembering important?

There will be moments in life when we are called to take action. We will be prompted to take steps of faith that make no sense to us. In remembering what God has done in our lives, we will be able to walk faithfully and obediently. We will be able to trust God when our journey is difficult.

Write out your own prayer thanking God for what He has done in your life, for what He is doing. Be as specific as you like.

DAY 5: SHARE YOUR STORY

Read 2 Kings 8:5-6.

As we begin today, let's take a moment to recap what has happened. A Shunammite woman who is childless has a room built for Elisha the prophet so that he may rest when he travels. To thank the Shunammite woman, Elisha says the woman will give birth to a son. She does give birth to a son but the boy dies a few years later. However, Elisha restores the boy to life and later warns the family they must leave because of a coming famine. Obediently, the family goes. Seven years later, they have returned and would like their land back.

In short, this Shunammite family completes a home renovation, births a child, loses that child, watches him raised back to life, moves suddenly, and returns and asks for their property back. Whew! Our sweet Shunammite sister has been on a journey! Reality television has nothing on this family's drama.

Now, it is time to reclaim their belongings.

Read the first part of 2 Kings 8:6. What does the woman do?

Our stories have value. Our stories encourage. They have the ability to draw others to our Savior.

Read John 4:7-26.

This passage details a beautiful interaction between Jesus and a Samaritan woman. Two facts are important here. In that day, a man would not speak to a woman he did not know. Furthermore, Jews did not speak to Samaritans. Here, Jesus reveals Himself, the Messiah, to a Samaritan woman. In fact, Jesus acknowledges the woman's sin while also speaking grace to her.

Now read John 4:39-42.

The Samaritan woman's story brought other Samaritans to Jesus! Had she not chosen to share her encounter with Jesus, the Samaritans would not have gone to Him. While in His presence, many more believed because of the words Jesus spoke. The Savior they once only heard about became the Savior they knew personally.

Your story and mine can have the same impact. Our stories can draw others to Him.

The places God has brought you out of, the impossible situations God has seen you through, the broken heart God has restored: all are stories worth being told. Knowing what God has done in your life and sharing it with others is vital for Kingdom growth.

We need to know we are not alone. We need to know others have been restored, redeemed, and made new.

Revelation 12:11 states:

> *They triumphed over him*
> *by the blood of the Lamb*
> *and by the word of their testimony;*
> *they did not love their lives so much*
> *as to shrink from death.*

If you have never shared your own story or testimony, consider it writing it out. Then, write the names of 1-3 people you will share your story with. If you are already comfortable sharing your story, pray for God to present opportunities for you to share with those who need to hear what God has done in your life.

A word of caution in telling your story: Choose people who are trustworthy. As Brené Brown says, "Share with people who have earned the right to hear your story." [3]

Week 3

THE WISE WOMAN OF ABEL

Then a wise woman called from the city, "Hear, hear! Please tell Joab, 'Come here that I may speak with you.'" So he approached her, and the woman said, "Are you Joab?" And he answered, "I am." Then she said to him, "Listen to the words of your maidservant." And he answered, "I am listening." Then she spoke, saying, "Formerly they used to say, 'They will surely ask advice at Abel,' and thus they ended the dispute. I am of those who are peaceable and faithful in Israel. You are seeking to destroy a city, even a mother in Israel. Why would you swallow up the inheritance of the Lord?"
— 2 Samuel 20:16-19

My friend, Katy, has an insane ability to make me feel both encouraged and smacked upside the head. In the nearly twenty years I have known her, I have yet to have a conversation with her without this happening. She stands secure in her faith. Katy points others towards Christ simply by being the woman she is. Being fully aware of how much time she spends in the Word and in communion with God, I know I can trust her. I trust her counsel and I trust her to keep private matters private. Katy is one of a handful of wise women God has placed in my life.

The wise woman of Abel speaks and saves her people. She is a woman of peace and of faith. She is a woman who has the courage to speak to Joab, a general of King David, as he pursues the rebel Sheba who had taken refuge in Abel.

She bravely speaks to Joab. Rather than sit idly by and watch her city be destroyed, this woman takes action to protect it. Joab then reveals his intentions to her.

> *Joab replied, "Far be it, far be it from me that I should swallow up or destroy! Such is not the case. But a man from the hill country of Ephraim, Sheba the son of Bichri by name, has lifted up his hand against King David. Only hand him over, and I will depart from the city." And the woman said to Joab, "Behold,*

> *his head will be thrown to you over the wall."*
> *(2 Samuel 20:20-21)*

Joab has no desire to hurt the innocent but seeks to protect King David. He is looking for the one responsible, and as this woman intercedes, Sheba is delivered to Joab.

> *Then the woman wisely came to all the people. And they cut off the head of Sheba the son of Bichri and threw it to Joab. So he blew the trumpet, and they were dispersed from the city, each to his tent. Joab also returned to the king at Jerusalem. (2 Samuel 20:22)*

This wise woman chose to speak and chose to take action. In doing so, the guilty one is found, innocent lives are saved, and peace is secured in the kingdom of David.

In a moment of crisis, a moment that would cause many to panic, this woman remains calm. She does not attack Joab but speaks with diplomacy and candor. She stops Joab from acting recklessly while persuading others to act justly.

A wise woman with a good reputation, whose name we do not know, acts courageously to be the voice for others.

Do you speak up to protect the innocent? Do you have a reputation that allows others to trust you? Do you use your position to help others?

DAY 1: WHAT'S IN YOUR HEART?

My husband and I have been intentional in teaching our daughter Scripture and in praying with her. When she experiences cruelty from others, we discuss forgiveness and what God's Word says. Over and over, we are teaching her the importance of not allowing lies and unforgiveness to take root in her mind or heart. We want her life to be filled with truth.

I have to believe that somewhere along the way the wise woman of Abel had truth and courage poured into her. Someone had to have told her the importance of living with integrity. This is the life she leads and what allows her to speak with boldness and confidence.

This is also why the voices we listen to matter. The Enemy would love nothing more than to fill our minds with lies. With expert subtlety, Satan will have us believing what is false, and have us convinced these are our own voices. The fact remains, if we fill our minds with junk, junk will spill out. If we fill our minds with truth, truth will pour out.

Read Luke 6:45 and summarize in the space provided.

What are ways you guard yourself against the junk, or lies, the enemy attempts to pour into you?

Think of the last time you were with a group of friends. Do you begin speaking or acting like them? I know I do. My mom once called me a people chameleon. I can quickly adapt my speech and mannerisms to those around me. While not inherently bad, I have to be careful to not lose sight of who God has called me to be. I must be intentional about where and with whom I spend my time.

Growing up, I struggled with anger. Truthfully, there was not much of a struggle; I was just angry. My internal anger led to speaking unkindly and to not treating people well. When I think of the words I spoke, I shudder. I knew the strength my words had, yet I freely spewed venom to any person who dared offend me.

Oh, but grace. Grace helped rewrite the story. The more I spent time with the Lord, in His Word, in prayer, in reading, and speaking with wise counsel, the more I was changed inwardly.

Week 3: The Wise Woman of Abel

Outwardly, my attitude and interactions with others also changed. My words changed because what was filling my heart changed.

Read Psalm 119:14-18.

Now, consider this: how often do you pray concerning what is in your heart? About what comes out of your mouth? How would this change if you were to pray over these things?

Read Proverbs 15:1-4.

Compare and contrast the tongue of the wise vs. the tongue of the fool.

Turn to Ephesians 4:29.

As you consider events from the past week, think of the words you spoke. Do the words you spoke cause you to cringe or smile? Explain.

Sister, I have experienced both. I will continue to have to tame my tongue. There are so many messages bombarding us and it can be a challenge to keep our hearts and mouths pure.

I want to be wise. Like the wise woman of Abel, I want people to hear any life-saving message I may have. I want my words to be trusted and filled with wisdom. You probably do too. How do we accomplish this?

Read Romans 10:8-10.

According to these verses, what results in salvation?

The heart and mouth are deeply intertwined because what is in one determines what comes out of the other. We must be careful what we allow ourselves to hear, see, and dwell upon.

- Spend time in the Word.
- Spend time in prayer.
- Find an accountability partner or group.
- Engage in a community of other believers.

I want your life to spill out Christ. I want to hear your praises in the way you speak to others. You can pour out wisdom and love, but you must first choose to be filled with them.

DAY 2: WORDS MATTER

My daughter has a friend who was experiencing physical illness because of what a classmate was saying to her. Day after day, unkind words were spoken. The stress caused by these words built until they overwhelmed the little girl and caused her stomach to become upset. A doctor's visit confirmed what the girl's mother thought, that stress from hearing negative words each day was the root of the illness. This incident proved to be a powerful lesson in the impact our words have on others.

We all know someone who can command a room. You know the one. When this person speaks, all go quiet. People lean in to hear what is being said. This person speaks honestly, openly, and for the benefit of others. This person's word can be trusted.

Isn't that how we should all strive to be? Too often, we are careless with our words. We do not restrain ourselves from our criticisms, our complaints, and joining in gossip. I have discovered not minding my words causes others to begin tuning me out. What happens then? Like the boy who cried wolf, no one bothers to listen regardless of the words spoken.

Read 2 Samuel 20:16-19 and summarize.

The Bible does not reveal the age of the wise woman of Abel. In my mind, she has greying hair, which is the reason Joab will listen to her. The fact is, we do not know for sure. We do know the woman does not mince words or soak Joab in flattery. I appreciate this woman's directness so very much.

You see, I live in the South where the phrase, "Bless 'em" supersedes any negative comment. This is the place where "we need to get together sometime" really means, "I am being nice, but I really do not want to spend any time with you, and have no plans of scheduling anything."

We are in a culture that smiles and nods then turns and blasts our venting on social media. Our actions prove our words cannot be trusted.

Read Proverbs 25:11-12.

What does this say words spoken at the right time are like?

Beautiful image, isn't it? Can you think of a time when words spoken to you felt this precious? Share below.

Now read Proverbs 18:20-21.

What lies in the power of the tongue?

The words we speak have consequences, either positive or negative. We need to be careful about what we allow to leave our lips.

Matthew 12:36-37 warns us concerning the words we speak: "But I tell you that everyone will have to give account on the day of judgment for every empty word they have spoken. For by your words you will be acquitted, and by your words you will be condemned."

Our words have power, great power, to either destroy or build up. How well do we choose on a given day? In our anger, what words do we allow to flow from our mouths? In our doubts and frustrations, what are we choosing to say? What kind of impact does it have on those who hear them?

The words we speak will tell others whether or not we can be trusted.

If you are like me, you have had less than stellar moments when you strung words together and hurled them carelessly like daggers. Maybe you have been prone to gossip, negativity, or unnecessary criticisms. If so, would you spend some time in prayer confessing these things? Pour out your heart to God. He will forgive and receive you with open arms. Ask Him to change your heart so that the words flowing from your mouth speak life and make you a person to whom others will listen.

DAY 3: KNOW YOUR MOTIVATION

There have been times that, more than anything, I had to prove I knew more, observed more, and had the better answer. It did not matter if I offended those around me, as long as I proved my point and swayed them to my beliefs. I wanted to be right and I wanted to be heard; those two desires drove my actions.

Thankfully, God has corrected my thinking in this area. Those desires still crop up from time to time, but my motivation has changed from wanting to be right and heard to wanting the other person to be drawn closer to God. Christ has refined my intentions, which alters my words and actions. Have you ever considered the "why" behind what you do? Why do you serve? Why did you defend someone? Why did you become angry? Why did you stay silent? Why did you speak? Regardless of the answer, invite Jesus to meet you in that place and take you to a place of healing.

In a moment of crisis, how do you respond? Do you take action or do you remain frozen in fear?

The wise woman of Abel intrigues me because the way she chooses to respond to the situation shows her desire to save her city. She speaks candidly to Joab without becoming rude or indignant. Why? Her city is in danger and she is aware that the safety of her people is at stake.

Turn to 2 Samuel 20 and read verses 19-21.

Why has Joab come to Abel? What does he want?

What happens in verse 22 of 2 Samuel 20?

Unlike Sheba, this wise woman keeps her head and keeps her city safe.

Many times, we are quick to react because we feel threatened. We become defensive and frantic in the face of trouble. If we were to keep in mind why we are responding as we are, we might be able to remain calm and handle the situation appropriately.

While we can easily fall into patterns of selfishness, we should strive to serve others: believers are motivated by God.

Read the following Scriptures: Psalm 40:8 and Psalm 73:25.

What is the motivation you see in these scriptures?

Ultimately, our motivation should be to please God and to serve others. Jesus describes this in Matthew 23:11-12, "The greatest among you shall be your servant. Whoever exalts himself will be humbled, and whoever humbles himself will be exalted."

In John 4:34, Jesus says, "My food is to do the will of Him who sent me and to accomplish His work."

This should be our goal as well: to accomplish His work.

Think of areas in which you serve. Why have you chosen these specific areas of service?

If you spend time reading the Bible or in prayer each day, why do you do so?

Why do you attend church? Bible study?

    I have a confession. While I take part in all of the activities mentioned above, there are times I perform them more out of routine and habit than out of a motivation to abide in my Heavenly Father. There are days I go through the motions, driven solely by the desire to say I have done each of them.

    I do not believe God is disheartened by this fact. He knows the nature of my heart, my wayward tendencies. Yet I also know that when my motivation is to dwell with my Father, to know Him and make Him known, my service and my time with Him is richer. These are the moments He draws me into the depths of who He is, and who He is calling me to be.

    Consider what motivates you in this life. Spend time in prayer and talk to God about these things. Ask Him to reveal any negative intentions driving you.

    Write your own prayer, or join me in praying:

Father, you are worthy of all praise and honor. My human heart and mind often wander and are filled with selfish desire. I do not always want to spend time reading, studying, or serving. I become sidetracked by my own ambitions. Forgive me for being led by selfishness. Change my heart and mind to be driven to follow you in obedience. Reveal to me any areas where my motivation is not pleasing to you. May my words and my life reflect your splendor.

Remember, more than participation in a Bible study or service in a particular area, God wants our hearts. Our love flows out of our connection to our Father.

I want to show love,

Not offer sacrifices,

I want you to know me,

More than I want burnt offerings.

(Hosea 6:6, NLT)

DAY 4: GIFTS ARE TO BE USED

Giving gifts is a true joy of mine. Having to wait to give the gifts, however, is not always my strong suit. I become so excited with what I have found for the recipient and want them to experience the joy of what the package holds as soon as possible.

I remember one year I found a great gift for my husband. His birthday was a week away, so I quickly wrapped his gift and sat it in the living room. His gift was in plain sight for the entire week before his birthday. And you know what? Not once did he notice it. The brightly wrapped box with the bow around it sat unnoticed on the floor for a week. When I presented it to him, I informed him where the gift had been the whole time: in plain sight! In his defense, he is the contemplative type; wrapping and bows do not always grab his attention. Yet what good is an unnoticed and unused gift?

What adjectives describe the woman of Abel in verses 19 and 22 of 2 Samuel 20?

This woman is gifted with wisdom. She knows how to approach Joab. She knows how to approach her people. She is wise and knows how to save her city. Our wise woman chooses to use her gifts. While things do not end well for Sheba, the people of Abel experience a positive outcome because of this woman's actions.

What gifts have you been given? How do you use them?

What, if anything, hinders you from using your gifts?

In my own life, fear has often kept me from using my gifts. Sometimes it is the lies spoken by the enemy that stop me. Rather than focusing on the gifts I have been given from the Creator of the universe, and on the truth, I turn my attention to the lies. It is

Week 3: The Wise Woman of Abel

only when I am aligned with truth that I am able to walk confidently in my gifts.

Read 1 Corinthians 12:6-11. List some of the gifts given.

Who gives these gifts?

In your own words, why has God given us various and different gifts?

Read 1 Corinthians 12:12-14, 27.

According to Scripture, we need one another's gifts for the body of Christ to be functional and effective. In order to work well we need to be using what God has given us. We benefit one another and glorify God by doing so.

In 1 Corinthians 12, the word "gift" in the Greek is *charisma*, meaning, "gracious favor granted." To further break down this word, *charis* means, "grace, a state of kindness and favor toward someone," often with a focus on a benefit given to the object.

As I discovered the meanings of those words, I came to understand our gifts are evidence of God's favor in our lives. Sister, we all have gifts. God did not just choose a few people to receive them. As we each use our gifts, we are showing favor to one another while glorifying God. Is that not incredible?

How does it change your perspective knowing the gifts given to you are God's way of extending grace and favor in your life?

Since using our gifts is a way we extend grace and favor to others, do you believe you will be less hesitant in using your gifts?

Week 3: The Wise Woman of Abel

Knowing these truths about how God has gifted me, I become excited when I have an opportunity to use them. I no longer compare my gifts to anyone else's because I have finally comprehended the value of what I have been given. Sister, using your gifts is a form of worship, of glorifying the heavenly Father. Let nothing hinder you. Go! Use your gifts!

DAY 5: BE AT PEACE

I once heard author and speaker Andy Andrews say to smile when you talk. He went on to say this one simple act would cause others to respond in kind. Since the moment Andrews uttered those words, I have done my best to smile when I talk whether face to face or over the phone with another person.

Standing in line at the grocery store one morning, I noticed the cashier seemed less than jovial. I, having heard Andy Andrews speak about the power of a smile, became determined to see this woman smile. As my turn came, I turned with a wide smile and exclaimed, "Good morning!" She did not smile. In fact, she responded by saying, "There is nothing good about it." I felt my smile faltering as she informed me what was wrong. One side of my mouth may have fallen. I did not want to leave the line with any negative words, however. With a smile I simply said, "I hope your day gets better and that you begin to feel better." Then, she smiled briefly at me and said, "Thank you."

It would have been easy to voice my own complaints. In fact, we often mimic the demeanor of the person whom we are speaking to. One person always adapts to the other. Have you ever started your day in a good mood only to see it turn sour after one poor conversation?

Romans 12:18 reads, "If possible, so far as it depends on you, be at peace with all men."

Be at peace with all men. Not only those I consider easy to be around, not solely my friends and those closest to me, but all people, like the grumpy cashier.

Sheba was not a man of peace. Based on 2 Samuel 20, he was a man causing problems. Our wise woman, however, wants to restore peace to her people. The chaos brought by Sheba is unwelcomed in the city of Abel.

How do you handle chaos when it arises in your life?

How do you react or respond when you encounter difficult people?

We have our own journeys. We have our trials, our struggles, our scars. We have wounds that threaten to drain the very life from us. We have moments of wondering if there is hope, if there really is an eternity waiting for us with open arms. We have stories we hold close because to even mention them would cause us to fall into the despair from which we have worked so hard to escape.

We have triumphs. We have moments that take our breath away at their sheer greatness. We pump our fists in excitement while attempting not to throw our victories tauntingly in front of one another. We rejoice with joy spilling over.

Our stories, our tragedies and our triumphs, shape us. They mold us into imperfect creatures living alongside one another, doing our best to be at peace with all people.

We fail. We do not respond how others need us. We unknowingly inflict wounds on one another as we seek to protect ourselves and protect the very ones with whom our lives collide. We want someone, anyone, to speak. We fear they will. We move between desperately wanting to share our story and wanting to keep it hidden close within us. We wonder why people won't speak. We are enraged when they do. We rejoice. We cry. We react.

As I read the story of Sheba, son of Bichri, I wonder what he experienced in life. I question the home he was raised in as well as the lessons he was taught. What caused him to raise his hand against King David? I wonder what decisions he made and if he was aware of the consequences of his actions.

Read the following Scriptures and note similarities you find among them:

Psalm 34:13-15

Psalm 37:10-12

Psalm 85:7-9

Proverbs 14:29-31

Peace is an extension of Christ.

We are wounded hearts muddling around, wanting to be noticed, to be seen, to be heard.

We live at peace with everyone when we come to see we are imperfect beings continually bumping into one another. We live at peace when we walk in grace. We can begin to extend grace as we realize each of us is doing his or her very best. We are struggling to survive in one moment and thriving in victory the next. We have stories we wish to leave behind because of how far we have come. We have scars from the roads we have traveled, pulsing red from exposure.

Recall a moment someone extended you grace that resulted in peace despite chaos happening around you. How did their response affect you?

Whether in line at a grocery store or within the walls of our own homes, we will encounter others who threaten to disturb our peace. Some individuals seem to thrive on chaos and disorder, but we do not have to choose to follow their lead. We do not have to pursue actions that will have others wanting to chop off our heads. We can choose peace.

How do you maintain peace in your own life? What habits do you have that promote peace?

We live in a world filled with turmoil. If we turn too much of our attention to what is happening around us, we can easily become entangled in worry and anxiety. But God is calling us to live at peace, with ourselves and with one another. Through Him and because of Him, peace is readily available.

Take a lesson from Sheba and do not lose your head.

Find a quiet place. Breathe deeply and slowly. Feel the muscles in your body relax. If it helps, play your favorite worship music. Fill your mind with the fact God is madly, deeply in love with you. He desires you to know Him intimately. He knows your name. He knows every worry. Spend time with Him and ask Him to restore peace in your heart.

Week 4

THE WIDOW AND THE JARS OF OIL

Elisha said, "Go around and ask all your neighbors for empty jars. Don't ask for just a few. Then go inside and shut the door behind you and your sons. Pour oil into all the jars, and as each is filled, put it to one side." — 2 Kings 4:3-4

An unnamed widow is left in debt, with two sons and one jar of oil. In her crisis, she cries out to the prophet Elisha. His instructions are simple, "*Gather jars and fill them.*"

In this moment of despair, this widow does not question. She acts. She tells her sons to go to the neighbors and to ask everyone whom they see. "*Gather jars and I will pour the oil.*" Jars were brought and oil was poured. More jars arrived; more oil was poured. As long as there were jars to fill, there was oil to fill them.

In her greatest time of need, her husband dead, and debt collectors threatening to take her sons as slaves, she sought advice from a man deeply connected to God. Elisha was a man who understood the limitless resources at God's disposal. The widow understood the advantage of wise, godly counsel. She knew he would help.

Elisha does not pay her debt for her but gives her a way to pay them herself.

Trusting the one from whom she sought help, she quickly responds. Using what she has in her possession, one jar of oil, a way is created to protect and care for herself and her sons. She sees only one jar of oil. Elisha, through God's wisdom, sees an opportunity to multiply and provide.

No other qualifications are needed; the widow uses what she already has.

How often do we think, "If I could do (insert gift or ability here), then I could accomplish (insert desired goal here)"? How many times have we spun our wheels seeing merely one jar of oil rather than the provision before us? We ask for help, but then doubt the answer. We see our problem, we shout "if only," and all the while fail to see the possibilities before us.

The dream in my heart was placed there for a reason. I am learning that everything I need to achieve it is already placed within me, or is within my reach. I remain stuck in my own doubts when action would bring the results I desire. Help will come and solutions will be found. My vision is sometimes so limited that I miss this simple fact.

God has provided all that I need, and He will continue to do so.

We lack because we do not ask. Elisha said not to ask for just a few. Our prayers are small and our belief even smaller. It is time. It is time to bring a multitude of super-sized jars for God to fill. That prayer you are scared to say because it looms too large? Say it to God! The desire of your heart that causes your heart to get caught in your throat? Ask for it!

As long as we bring the jars, He will be faithful to fill them.

Week 4: The Widow and the Jars of Oil

What prayers have you been hesitant to ask? Are you bringing every jar possible for God to fill? How would your life and your faith change by obediently bringing every jar God provides?

DAY 1: BRING THE JARS

Our church's college group ventured to a ropes course for our fall retreat. We spent time climbing, jumping, team building, and laughing. It was a beautiful weekend, perfect for our scheduled adventures.

We followed our instructor around the course, arriving at a large platform. He instructed one person to stand on the platform, and for everyone else to form two lines facing one another with arms outstretched and interlaced. The individual on the platform was then told to cross her arms across her chest and fall backwards. What an entertaining exercise: catching person after person, watching the look in their eyes move from fear to joy. It was so fun until it was my turn.

As I climbed onto the platform, I made a comment about being okay with this exercise since all the males in our group were waiting below. I regretted speaking my thought aloud when the instructor faced the two lines below us and said, "Guys, step out of the line. Girls, you stay there, fill in the gaps, and make sure your arms are interlocked." He expected me to trust the group of women standing on the ground. I thought he must have lost his mind. I did not believe they would catch me.

Week 4: The Widow and the Jars of Oil

Read 2 Kings 4:1-7 and describe the situation.

A woman's husband has died, leaving his family with debt. Those he owed money to threaten to take the woman's sons as slaves in order to work off the debt.

The widow goes into protection mode. She is grieving her husband and does not want to lose her sons as well. My mama's heart pounds as I read through this story.

The widow asks Elisha for help. Elisha gives her instructions: what are they (2 Kings 4:3-4)?

Gather jars and fill them. Our widow does.

Charles Spurgeon had this to say about the widow and the jars of oil:

My conviction is, Brethren, that we do not pray enough. I do not, by this remark, measure our prayers by time but I mean that we do not ask enough of God. We are not straitened in Him but we are often straitened in ourselves. The Prophet's advice to the woman was, "Borrow empty vessels" – notice the next word –

88 Unnamed Women of the Bible

"borrow not a few." It was needful, thus to urge her to large things. Covetous men need restraining but in asking of the Lord, our hearts need enlarging.

This godly widow had the blessing now at her disposal to increase or diminish. If she borrowed few vessels, she would have but little oil. If she borrowed many vessels they should all be filled and she should have much oil. She was herself to measure out what she should have. And I believe that you and I, in the matter of spiritual blessings from God, have more to do with the measurement of our mercies than we think. We make our blessings little, because our prayers are little.[4]

I sometimes wonder what size these jars were. In my mind, they are more like large vats. This woman is recently widowed with two children, in debt, and living in a society that does not value women. Yes, give me the barrels to fill with oil to ensure there is enough for the rest of our days on earth. I would want large barrels, and lots of them.

As long as the jars were brought, there was oil to fill them. And I wonder, what kind of jars am I bringing before God? What prayers am I praying? Safe? Timid? Doubt-filled? Or big, vat-sized prayers?

God desires to fill us with so much good we can barely contain it. Yet, we question if we are being too greedy, too selfish, want too much, or even if we are deserving at all. When God says to fill the jars, and gives no other instructions, fill as many as possible!

Take a moment. What is a prayer you have been hesitant to pray? Write it here.

What do you believe has caused your hesitation?

Trust. Most often, we have a trust issue. As I stood on the platform being told to cross my arms and fall backwards, I struggled with my conviction that the women below would catch me. However, they did. I did not enjoy the activity but it did help me to see my own trust issue.

We wonder if God can truly be trusted. We seem to know He is able, but we are not sure He will come through. In order to protect our hearts, to avoid disappointment, we pray safe, small prayers.

Read the following verses and write down what they reveal to you about prayer.

Matthew 7:7-8

Matthew 21:21-22

James 5:17-18

Recall a time you prayed for something specific and God answered. Write about it and recall what you thought and felt. Remind yourself God is able.

Spurgeon also says:

We have a great many cares, cares about our boys and girls, cares about our business, cares about household concerns. But we do not bring these cares to God – we feel as if they were too little to mention to Him.

This is so absurd that I will have no more to do with such sinful silences. Let us tell it all to Jesus. Or else the case stands thus – you have your empty vessels and you will not bring them to be filled. Why will you be so wickedly foolish? When the Lord bids you cast your care upon Him, for He cares for you, why not cast it there? Why will you carry your sin, your need, your care? These cares are different sets of empty vessels for the Grace of God to fill. Oh, why, my Brethren, why have we not larger desires and broader expectations, that according to our faith it may be done unto us?[5]

What big prayer are you ready to pray?

DAY 2: THE OBEDIENCE BLESSING

"Obedience does not always mean it will be easy," he stated. The man sitting before me was a trusted friend and wise mentor. I smiled, knowing he spoke from his own experiences. The obedient step he and his wife were taking would put miles between them and their extended family. It was the right step, the one to which God had called them, but it was difficult. I smiled as he further shared with me, "Yes, but there is always blessing in obedience."

Read 2 Kings 4: 3-4. What does Elisha tell the widow to do? In verse 5, how does she respond?

Notice the widow does not question Elisha. She does not call her mom, her sister, her best friend to gather opinions on how sound the advice Elisha has given her is. She simply begins gathering the jars.

Week 4: The Widow and the Jars of Oil

Read 2 Kings 4:6-7. What is the result?

Can you recall a time your obedience has led to a blessing? Share below.

One summer, I felt God telling me to set aside a business opportunity. This opportunity had been benefitting my family; I believed strongly in the company and the possibilities it provided. However, God was clear. Two weeks later I finally obeyed, and I was blown away as God began to unfold opportunities and lessons. My obedience led to writing this study, to becoming involved in ministry in a way that excites me, and so much more.

Why is obedience important?

Read Romans 6:16-18. In essence, what does obedience to God result in?

Obedience sets us free from sin. Bondage is no more.

The widow's obedience to Elisha's directions leaves her with enough oil to pay off her family's debts. She also has enough oil for personal use. God's supply matched the widow's faith and obedience.

How many times have we prayed or even begged for a solution, only to complain when we received the answer? I have. I have found myself pleading, but when the answer required much of me, I rebelled, fought, acted like a spoiled child.

How beautiful to have the faith and obedience of this widow. She knows what is required of her. She does not look for an easier way out, or for someone else to do all the work. Every vessel collected is used.

The excuses for our disobedience are easy to list. Every one of them starts with our excuses.

But I can't.

But I am not able.

But I don't know enough.

Week 4: The Widow and the Jars of Oil

But I am not accomplished enough.

But I don't do that kind of thing.

But that is outside my norm, my comfort zone, my self-determined limitations.

But Moses said to God, "Who am I that I should go to Pharaoh and bring the Israelites out of Egypt?" (Exodus 3:11)

But Moses said, "Pardon your servant, Lord. Please send someone else." (Exodus 4:13)

Moses' excuses and fears got in the way. He would lead the Israelites to the land God promised, but he would not set foot in it. Instead he would see it in the distance from atop the mountain where he would breathe his last.

I know I too will miss walking fully in the promises intended for me if I do not trust, if I do not believe. And I? I want to see all God has both for me and for those around me.

Like the widow with the jars of oil, let us go about collecting as many as we are able for God to fill. He will be faithful as we walk in obedience.

If there is an area you have not been obedient in, confess it here. Ask God to help you bring every jar possible for Him to fill. Ask Him to help you believe that the task before you is possible.

DAY 3: ASK FOR HELP

My crutches went sailing across the room. I had thrown them in my frustration. A second ankle surgery had me hobbling around in pain, unable to do my normal everyday tasks. I sat there crying, annoyed at what I could not do. My body was not healing well because I had not been resting as instructed. But who had time? There was a to-do list and daily chores to tackle.

As my husband entered the room and quickly assessed the situation, he knelt beside me and asked, "What can I do to help you?" The floodgate opened as I listed out all the chores needing to be done, and how overwhelmed I felt. He reminded me he was there to help me, but I would have to ask because he could not read my mind (which is probably a good thing).

Read 2 Kings 4:1-2. What help does the woman need?

In verse 7, what is the result of the help the widow has been given?

Week 4: The Widow and the Jars of Oil

Is there a problem you are facing with which you need help?

What keeps you from asking for help?

    We all have moments in which we must ask this question. *Will you help me? I have been trying to do this alone and it is not working. Help. Please.* Some find the act of reaching out to someone else to be easy; others struggle and resist until they are nearly shattered.

    What is the cause of our hesitancy? Pride? Shame?

    In my own life, I have seen my own lack. I have been embarrassed at what I could not do on my own. Fearing I might be deemed unfit, I became an expert in false pretenses. *Yes, I am fine. Nothing bothers me. I am strong. I need no one.*

    Pride consumed me and a heart of stone began to form.

    With great care, I constructed a wall, carefully choosing what others would see and hear. They saw the smile and heard the jokes. Rarely did the truth find its way from behind the stones.

How many times did I want to flip a switch and have help appear before me? How many times did I long to be noticed, for the hurt and the struggle to be revealed? How often did I want to crumble from the pressure of those stones?

Grace: persistent, beautiful grace stood by.

Through friendships, in mentors, in words spoken to me, Grace began deconstructing the barriers. Grace saw beyond the stony wall. Grace chiseled away at the hardest of places.

Grace met me in the raw, barren moments filled with the hurt and anger and insecurities I had long held. Grace began rearranging the terrain.

Pride gave way to humility. Humility caused my hand to reach out to those around me. Humility had me asking the question I most feared. *Will you help me?* Grace and humility revealed the beauty in fellowship and community.

However, there are times we ask the wrong people for help and we end up in a far worse situation. The widow asks Elisha for help, a man of God, a man who could be trusted and was concerned with the welfare of others.

Thinking of the problem you listed above, is there a person you can think of who is properly equipped to help you?

Read 2 Kings 4:3-5. Where do the vessels come from?

There will be times the best we can do is pray, and reach out to those who have what we need. There are people willing to help, to fill the needs of others, if only they knew the need existed!

Notice the widow and her sons did not wait for the jars to be brought to them. They had to go ask for them, retrieve them, and receive the help given.

Are you stuck in fear and unwilling to go outside of your area of comfort to ask for help?

In asking for help, we allow others to use their gifts. Let us not become trapped into thinking we should walk by ourselves with the world on our shoulders. We were each created with a purpose, as a part of one body. Helping allows the body to function properly.

We were not meant to do this life alone. We were created for fellowship. True fellowship, or *koinonia*, will have us both reaching out for help and helping others.

DAY 4: HE WILL EQUIP YOU

Beginning the certification process to be a Life Purpose Coach was thrilling. I dove into the assignments and listened to testimonies of how life coaching had helped people. I received great information, but I was not ready to be someone's life coach. It was not until I began receiving various tools during coaching that I started to understand how the process worked. As my notebook of resources grew and I learned how to use them appropriately, my confidence in being a life coach also grew.

My mentor made sure to fully equip me to coach others effectively.

The widow was in a desperate place. She was not prepared to accomplish the task of caring for her family and paying off their debt. She was now responsible to meet the demands of the creditors and care for her sons.

Oh, but grace. God, rich in mercy and grace, equipped her to succeed along with the help of others.

Have you faced a situation for which you felt unequipped? Describe it below.

God often leaves me in awe of how He works. After this long in my faith journey, maybe I should no longer be surprised, but I stand in childlike wonder quite often.

Scripture tells us God will equip us. If you are like me, you need reminders every now and then when you question how He might prepare you.

Read the following verses and list what each means to you, noting how God equips us.

Hebrews 13:21

Philippians 2:13

It is by God working in and through us that we become equipped. He keeps his promises, and as we walk in faith, He provides all we need along the journey. Through past experiences, mentors, and time with Him, we can successfully walk the road before us.

I am reminded of Queen Esther and how God equipped her, a Hebrew woman, to go before the king in order to save her people. If you have not read her story, I encourage you to do so. Esther is a woman of courage and dignity; she is brave and beautiful. When she goes to the king without being summoned, as was customary, she is not punished. Instead, she is welcomed. God protects her. He has given her a place in the palace, married to the king: the one who can protect Esther's people from an evil man's plans.

Read Ephesians 6:10-18. We are equipped when we are rooted in truth, when we carry the right tools. List the armor of God. Which portion of God's armor do you tend to forget?

DAY 5: COMMUNITY WINS

I am thankful the widow could not save herself. She had to ask for help and rely on others in order to gather the vessels Elisha instructed her to gather. She could not do it alone.

My independent, stubborn heart needs this lesson. I often rely entirely on myself regardless of how I long to have others walk with me.

How important is community to you?

In his poem *Mending Wall*, Robert Frost says good fences make good neighbors. Maybe he is right. Sometimes, though, I am unsure. While a fence allows us to respect one another's property, it also keeps us more distant from one another. In many regards, fences are good. But how do fences function in the face of our need for community? We were created to be in fellowship with one another. We were created to live and work alongside others.

So what of these barriers we place between others and ourselves? These fences we erect should not be intended to shut people out. Through the gate we welcome them, into the safety of the boundaries we have created. Come, sit a while, you will be safe here.

But we must be willing to open the gate. It is sometimes too easy and too comfortable to remain in our dreams of a house with the white picket fence, stable and secure. But staying inside never allows us to grow and commune.

My heart longs for community. The fences are fine and often necessary. But I want gates with well-oiled hinges, ready to swing wide to allow entrance to another. I want a heart willing to unlatch the gate, to welcome others. I want them to feel welcome inside the walls we have built. Even if they do not desire to come, I want them to always know they are invited.

We can even find community online now. As a part of a few online communities, there are days I am overwhelmed with all the noise. Other days, those communities offer me a safe place filled with endless encouragement.

Scripture supports the concept of community. Read the following passages and note what each says about community.

Hebrews 10:24-25

Acts 2:42-47

Galatians 6:2

Ecclesiastes 4:9-12

Why then is community important?

Community encourages, supports, and protects its members. We are strengthened by one another.

Depending on your personality, actively engaging in community may be uncomfortable. Please do not misunderstand: I am not saying we need to bring in the masses and all become extroverts who freely speak to each one of our neighbors. We do need others, however. We need to be connected to a body of believers, communing with one another. We need the gifts they have. We need the support, the accountability, and the prayers.

List 3-5 people you consider your community. Then, thank the Lord for each of those people. Also, consider writing these individuals a card letting them know how valued they are.

A FINAL WORD

Friend, thank you for journeying with me the last four weeks. It has been an honor to walk alongside of you. Were you able to identify with these four magnificent women? Did you see your own story in theirs? As I studied and as I wrote, I certainly did.

These unnamed women have shown me how deeply God loves His daughters. Though we often feel unheard, unseen, or forgotten, God knows us fully. He knows us by name. I would have no great joy than for you to know God is renaming us:

Guilty, you are now Forgiven.

Forgotten, you are now Remembered.

Dirty, you are now Clean.

Hopeless, you are now Hope-filled.

Unknown, you are now Known.

Desperate, you are now Secure.

Betrayed, you are now Redeemed.

Depressed, you are now Joyful.

Fearful, you are now Peaceful.

Broken, you are now Restored.

Unworthy, you are now Daughter of the Most High King.

Discussion Guide

Week 1

1. What lesson, exercise, etc., impacted you the most from week 1? Explain as much as you are comfortable with.
2. What does it mean to you to be called God's Daughter?
3. What lie is God helping you to overcome?
4. What intrigues you about the woman with the issue of bleeding?
5. What does it mean to you to know God sees you and God hears you?
6. Are you seeking restoration in an area of your life? Has God restored an area of your life? Share what you are comfortable sharing with your group.

WEEK 2

1. In studying the Shunammite woman, what did you enjoy most?
2. What is one lesson you learned from her?
3. Share ways you remember what God has done.
4. How do you cultivate contentment in your life?
5. Why is sharing your story important to you? What frightens you about sharing your story? How can we encourage one another as we share?

WEEK 3

1. What lesson, exercise, etc, impacted you the most from this week?
2. In what ways do you guard your heart?
3. How have the words you said or the words spoken to you affected your life?
4. How do you ensure your actions are being taken with the correct motivation?
5. What gifts have you been given and how are you using them?
6. How do you maintain peace in your own life?

WEEK 4

1. What lesson from the woman and the jars of oil stood out to you the most?
2. What jars is God asking you to bring to Him?
3. What keeps you from being obedient to God's leading? What blessings have you experienced as a result of your obedience?
4. Why do you believe we struggle with asking others for help?
5. How important is community to you? What function does community serve in your life? Your family's?

Acknowledgements

I am forever thankful God called me to pen these words. He is the reason I write, the reason I teach, the Savior for whom I am eternally grateful. Thank you, Father, for trusting me with these lessons for your daughters.

Andy, you spoke life into this dream long before I dared to. Thank you for encouraging me to continue writing, to go forward with the idea to teach this to others, and for helping me dream big, scary dreams. I am so happy to walk beside you in this life. Thank you for choosing me to be your bride.

Zoe, sweet girl, you are the greatest teacher I have ever known. You speak wisdom far beyond your years, and your kindness amazes me. It is an honor and privilege to be your mom. Thank you for all the times you looked at me and said, "You are the best." I think you are extraordinary.

Dad, Mom, Jen, I love you. Thank you for being the greatest family a girl could ask for. You make life wonderful.

Katy McCulloch, Kristi McLelland, Pastor Chris Williamson, Pastor Paige Allen, Pastor Doug Halcomb, Kimberly Coronel, Strong Tower Bible Church, and Live Oak Community Church, you have been wise teachers and offered me wise counsel.

I have grown and learned from you in exceptional ways. Thank you for speaking truth and for caring deeply about seeing others flourish in their faith.

Ron Reynolds and Jan Loy, for being the first to call me a writer. Your wisdom and encouragement have breathed life into my weary soul. Rick Loy, I lean into your every word. Thank you for sharing your wisdom.

An enormous thank you to Erica Waggoner and Jill Dyer. Yours were the first eyes to see this study in its completion. Each week you were faithful to edit, add valuable input, and challenge me to go deeper. Thank you for wanting this to be great, for being honest, and for challenging me to be better. Your insights and edits blew me away. This study is stronger and better because of you. I am forever grateful.

Bethany Beams, you are a rock star, a genius, and a gem. Thank you for using your gifts so wonderfully. How you created such beautiful designs when I did not know what I wanted baffles me. Thank you for being willing to walk this road with me.

Jami Clinton, LeCreshia Phillips, Julie Haverdink, Kelly Lokey, Becca Rotan, Carey Martin, Heather Schultz, Josie Brumbalow, and Christine Fryoux: thank you for being faithful friends and prayer warriors. Thank you for talking me off the ledge of insanity, and for not pushing me right over.

Rick Theule, the big brother I never had. Thank you for being a sounding board and constant encourager. You will never know how appreciative I am.

The Unnamed Women of the Bible trial group: Carley, Caroline, Carrie, Christy, Debbie, Denise, Julie, Kelly, Liz, Mary Ellen, Mandi, Olivia, and Tina. Thank you for saying yes to walking through this study. Thank you for allowing me to stumble my way through this with you, to test out my ability to teach to a group of incredible women. Your part in this journey is invaluable. Truly, you are beautiful daughters of the Holy King.

Thank you Internet Café Devotions team and Suzanne Eller, for allowing me to share my words and my story on incredible platforms. You have strengthened me and helped me to become better.

To all the dreamers and builders, the ones who are out living their lists, for women living free, and launch teams, thank you for cheering loudly and often for me during this endeavor. At just the right times, you spoke hope and life into this dream of mine. Thank you.

To all who will read this study, thank you. Thank you for walking through these four weeks. I pray you are encouraged and have found how deeply valued and treasured you are. You are God's precious daughter.

Notes

1. Chesterton, G.K., *A Miscellany of Men*, (Kessinger Publishing, 2004), p. 106.
2. Bell, Rob, *Velvet Elvis: Repainting the Christian Faith*, (Harper Collins, 2012).
3. Brown, Brené, *Daring Greatly: How the Courage to Be Vulnerable Transforms the Way We Live, Love, Parent, and Lead*, (Penguin Publishing Group, 2012).
4. Charles H. Spurgeon, Sermon 2063, "The Filling of Empty Vessels," in *Spurgeon Gems & Other Treasures of God's Truth*, ed. Emmett O'Donnell, Eternal Life Ministries, accessed April 13, 2015, http://spurgeongems.org/vols34-36/chs2063.pdf
5. Ibid.

Made in United States
North Haven, CT
12 July 2025